AUSTRALIAN
SNAKES

Belinda Edwards was born into a farming family,
and the words that echoed throughout her childhood
every time she left the house were 'watch for snakes'.
Don't go into the hay shed there will be snakes.
Be careful down by the river there will be snakes.
But she was never actually told what to do if she was
bitten. As an adult, finding these words still ringing
in her ears, she decided to find out for herself.
Unable to find a book that suited her needs,
she decided to write her own.

E lliot Puckett

The Five Mile Press Pty Ltd
1 Centre Road, Scoresby
Victoria 3179 Australia
www.fivemile.com.au

Text copyright © Belinda Edwards 2003, 2009
Photographs copyright © Melbourne Reptile House and Ray Hoser

This edition published by The Five Mile Press Pty Ltd, 2009
First published in 2003 by Pennon Publishing

Printed in China
Cover design by Kristy Lund
Page design by Allan Cornwell and Caz Brown
Illustrations by Neil

National Library of Australia Cataloguing-in-Publication entry:

Author:	Edwards, Belinda, 1961–
Title:	Australian snakes : a pictorial guide / Belinda Edwards.
Edition:	Rev. ed.
ISBN:	9781742116181 (pbk.)
Subjects:	Snakes—Australia
Dewey Number:	597.96

AUSTRALIAN
SNAKES
A PICTORIAL GUIDE

BELINDA EDWARDS

The Five Mile Press

Contents

All snakes are protected in Australia. If you need to have a snake removed because it is posing a threat, you should contact a licensed snake handler. You will find them on the internet, or you can contact your state department responsible for wildlife.

Introduction

Australian Snakes: A Pictorial Guide is an easy-to-read guide for students, bushwalkers and anyone interested in learning more about Australian snakes.

It looks in detail at over forty of Australia's most well known and colourful snakes, describing their features, characteristics and habitats. It includes full-colour photographs and distribution maps.

Australian Snakes describes the basics of snake anatomy, their senses, reproductive methods, movement and feeding habits. It looks at snakebites and how to prevent them, and provides the most current first-aid measures available. Hotline numbers for both bites and venom are provided at the back.

This slimline production is perfect for bushwalks and camping trips. But, remember, most snakes are dangerous. Do not take risks, and never handle snakes.

PART 1
ABOUT THE SNAKE

Basic snake anatomy

Windpipe
The windpipe carries air to the lungs. It is strengthened by cartilaginous (flexible) ribs so that it maintains its shape even when the snake eats very large prey.

Heart
The heart is very powerful because it must push the blood to the end of the snake; in some snakes that can be 10 metres or more.

Oesophagus
The muscle bands of the oesophagus contract sequentially to propel food down to the stomach.

Saccular lung
Most snakes have only a single useful lung. The other is greatly reduced in size.

Stomach
The stomach is a muscular tube that can expand to take very large prey.

Small intestine
Like all other carnivores, snakes have a very simple digestive tract.

Hemipenis
Male snakes have two penises which lie inverted in the base of the tail when not in use. Only one penis is used at a time.

Testes
These consist of many convoluted tubes. The sperm is stored in the sperm duct until needed, then moved down a tube to the hemipenis.

Kidneys
Like most other organs in the snake, the kidneys are elongated and positioned one above the other.

Rectum
Faeces are excreted from the snake's rectum.

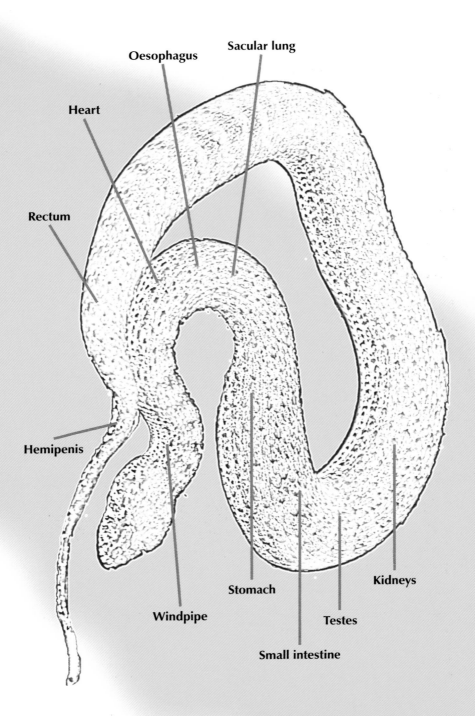

Heart

Oesophagus

Sacular lung

Rectum

Hemipenis

Windpipe

Stomach

Small intestine

Testes

Kidneys

The senses

- All snakes have an excellent sense of smell.

- A snake flicks its tongue in and out as it moves along to pick up particles from the ground, which are then transferred to the sensitive smelling organs in the roof of its mouth.

- A snake can also smell through its nostrils, but not very well.

- All snakes are completely deaf.

- Snakes detect movement through vibrations.

- Snakes cannot see very well and will not notice an object unless it moves.

- Snakes have no eyelids. This causes them to stare.

- Snakes' eyes are covered with a transparent scale.

- During the shedding of the skin, eye scale becomes opaque and the snake's vision becomes clouded.

The skin

In warm weather snakes slough (shed) their outer skins quite regularly.

Sloughing occurs more frequently with younger snakes.

General sloughing occurs in the following sequence:

1. The scale covering the eye becomes cloudy, and when this clears (2 to 3 days normally) the snake will find a rough object to rub against in order to remove its old skin.

2. The skin over the jaws and lips is pulled back over the head.

3. The whole of the old skin is then turned inside out (like pulling off a sock).

A snake which has recently shed its skin is usually at its most colourful.

The skin of a snake is not slimy as is often believed. It is quite dry.

Movement

- Snakes are generally slow-moving creatures, but can move at speed in short bursts.

- The spine of a snake consists of between 180 and 400 vertebrae. A snake does not have a chest bone.

- A snake has a pair of ribs attached to each vertebra by a ball-and-socket joint. The number of vertebrae and the manner in which the ribs are attached give the snake its flexibility.

- As a snake moves forward, each part of the body follows the same course as the body part directly in front, giving its movement that effortless gliding manner.

- A snake's maximum continuous speed on level ground is seven kilometres per hour.

- A snake moves forward by friction with the surface; it has difficulty moving on smooth surfaces.

- Although their speed along the ground is generally slow, snakes have the ability to quickly pivot around any point of the body (especially if they are being held).

- All snakes can swim.

Reproduction

- It is generally accepted that in Australia only the Taipan, the Small-scaled Snake, the brown snakes and the Mulga are oviparous (egg laying). All other species are viviparous (live bearing).

- Some live births may take place in a thin filmy sac from which the young quickly emerge.

Identification

- For most snakes, positive identification can only be made by the counting of body scales and examination of the head shield and anal plate.

- Using colour as a means of identification is unreliable because of variation.

The fangs

- The fangs of dangerous venomous snakes are thin, sharply pointed and hollow.

- Venom is produced in glands, which can be found in the side of the head, behind the eyes.

- The venom passes from the glands into a canal running through to the tip of the fang.

- During a bite, muscles around the venom glands contract to control the amount of venom injected.

- Large amounts of venom are injected by some snakes as they chew on their prey.

- The more flexible the fangs are (i.e. their ability to rotate) the more venomous the snake is.

- New fangs are grown from time to time during the life of a snake.

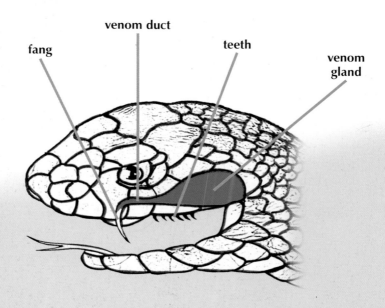

venom duct · fang · teeth · venom gland

The venom

- Venom enables a snake to paralyse its prey quickly and efficiently so it can be easily swallowed.

- Australian snake venoms contain neurotoxins – proteins which affect the nerve endings and muscles of their prey. These cause paralysis and an inability to breathe.

- Snake venoms may contain a number of other dangerous proteins. One component can prevent blood from clotting, so the prey bleeds to death.

- Some proteins help the venom to spread away from the bite, thus quickly affecting other nerve endings and muscles.

- Australian snakes produce a lot of venom. The average amount of venom contained by a Taipan at any one time is enough to kill 10,000 small rodents.

A Death Adder from Queensland preparing to devour a pigeon

Feeding habits

Snakes swallow their prey headfirst so that limbs or feathers flatten against the victim's body, making swallowing easier.

The lower jaw of a snake can dislocate while its prey is being swallowed. This allows the snake to swallow quite large rodents and birds. A snake relocates its jaw with a number of opening and closing movements.

A snake's brain is completely surrounded by bone, which gives protection against victims that struggle when being swallowed.

A number of teeth situated behind the snake's fangs curve backwards, preventing the victim from coming back out of the snake's mouth.

Because it is cold blooded, a snake generally only feeds when the ambient temperature of the environment allows the digestive juices in the stomach to work effectively. If the temperature drops, digestion will slow; if digestion stops, a snake can die when the swallowed prey ferments inside the stomach. This is a common cause of snake death in captivity if cage temperature is not maintained correctly.

Bits of the prey such as tough skin, rough hair and claws are often not completely digested and are either excreted or regurgitated.

Snakebites

Symptoms of snakebite

- Headache

- Nausea

- Vomiting

- Abdominal pain

- Collapse

- Unconsciousness

- Painful, tender muscles

- Blurred or double vision

- Difficulty in swallowing or breathing

- Slurred speech

- Weakness

- Pins and needles in limbs

Taipan – Australia

Signs of snakebite

Puncture marks, usually on limbs, which may consist of single or double puncture or scratch marks, but are often difficult to see

Multiple punctures from severe bite

Tenderness and/or swelling of the lymph nodes (this may also be caused by a non-venomous bite)

Bleeding or oozing

Dark urine

Sleepiness, paralysis, weakness

Breathing difficulties

Cardiac arrest

Irritability, confusion, coma

Preventing snakebite

- Leave snakes alone. Normally a snake will try to avoid confrontation with people.

- Do not attempt to handle snakes.

- Never put hands inside logs, thick grass, or under woodpiles or building materials without looking first.

- When stepping over logs look first.

- Keep sheds and barns mice free. They attract snakes.

- Keep grass well cut.

- Most bites happen when snakes are trodden on or touched while sleeping. The snake then tries to defend itself.

- Bushwalkers should always carry a pressure bandage. You don't want to be 10 kilometres away from one if someone gets bitten.

- It is important to wear stout shoes and sensible clothing in country where there may be snakes. Bushwalkers who walk in shorts often wear long socks and gaiters for protection.

- Snakes are very active on warm summer nights and it is advisable to keep a torch handy when camping.

- If bitten, seek medical attention immediately.

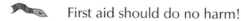

First aid

Basic principles

There are several important principles which should guide proper administration of first aid.

- First aid should do no harm!

- First aid should be practical and achievable.

- First aid should be based on current clinical methods and scientific knowledge.

Older 'first aid' methods for snakebite are examples of techniques which have the potential to cause the patient harm. For example, the use of tourniquets and the old classic of cutting the bite and sucking out the poison have caused permanent injuries and even death.

The pressure immobilisation method

The pressure immobilisation method of treating snakebites was developed by Dr Struan Sutherland and the Commonwealth Serum Laboratories in Melbourne in 1978. It is based on an understanding of the structure of snake toxins.

The aim of Sutherland's pressure immobilisation method is to retard the spread of venom through the lymphatic system. This is achieved in two ways.

Firstly, the lymphatic vessels at the site of the bite are compressed by immediately bandaging around the bite site. Bandaging the rest of the bitten limb as soon as possible further reduces the spread of the toxin.

Secondly, the spread of the toxin through the lymph system is slowed or stopped by applying a splint to the limb. This has the effect of stopping the muscles pumping blood around the body.

If correctly applied, this technique can stop venom movement through the system without damage to limb tissue – one of the problems encountered when using tourniquets.

Treating snakebite with the pressure immobilisation method

Important note: this method is only first aid. It is not a proper medical treatment for snakebite. Medical assistance should be sought as soon as possible. Most hospitals are equipped with antivenom. After initial tests and precautions have been taken, all first aid will be removed and the bite treated with antivenom.

Apply a firm broad bandage over the site of the bite. Use whatever clothing is available for this purpose – shirts are ideal. Use the same sort of pressure as you would for bandaging a sprain. Do not bandage too tightly as this can totally prevent circulation and damage muscles and limbs.

Once the bite site has been bandaged, apply additional bandages over as much of the rest of the bitten limb as you can. If the removal of clothing will disturb the bitten limb, it is better to bandage over the clothing.

Make sure the bitten limb is kept immobile by applying a splint and keeping the patient as quiet and still as possible. Bring transport to the victim.

The pressure immobilisation method of first aid is ideal for bites by all Australian species of snake. Turn over to see a diagram.

Applying a pressure immobilisation bandage

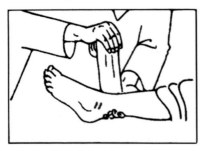

1. Apply a broad pressure bandage over the bite area. Keep the patient still – do not take off clothing as this will speed up the movement of venom into the bloodstream.

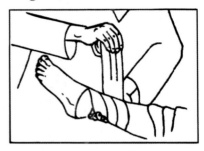

2. Make the bandage tight.

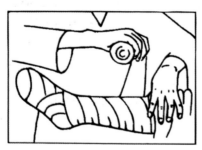

3. Extend the bandage as far as possible.

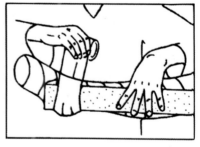

4. Apply a splint.

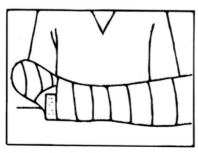

5. Bind it firmly to the limb.

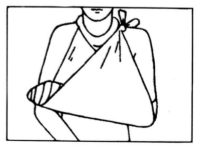

6. If the bite is on hand or arm, put limb in a sling.

Do's and don'ts

Do's

Keep the patient still and reassure them.

Maintain vital functions.

Immediately apply a pressure immobilisation bandage.

Keep the patient as still as possible and bring transport to them as quickly as possible.

Seek medical help at the earliest opportunity.

If the snake has been killed, bring it with the patient.
Do not waste time, risk further bites or delay the application of a pressure bandage and splint by trying to kill the snake.

Don'ts

Do not wash the wound. Venom left on the skin can be used to identify the snake so that the correct antivenom can be used.

Do not use a tourniquet.

Do not cut or suck the wound.

Do not give alcohol to the patient.

PART 2

SNAKE TYPES

Children's Python

Antaresia childreni

Family: *Boidae*
Genus: *Antaresia*
[Gray, 1842]

Body: thick
Head: semi-broad
Colour:
> *Body* – light brown with lighter coloured sides with irregular dark purplish-brown blotches along the back
> *Head* – light brown with darker flecks or blotches, dark streak through the eye
> *Belly* – creamish to light brown
> *Eyes* – a dark streak through each eye

Length: up to 1.5 metres; average 0.75 metres
Non-venomous: not dangerous
Habitat: from coastal to desert
Young: egg laying

Description:
Commonly referred to as a Carpet Snake, the Children's Python has heat-sensitive pits on its lower jaw to help find and track prey. It is secretive and well camouflaged. Being mainly nocturnal, it feeds upon small mammals, birds and reptiles. Often it inhabits empty burrows. It is the second smallest of the pythons and is a popular pet.

28

Spotted Python

Antaresia maculosa

Family: *Boidae*
Genus: *Antaresia*
[Peters, 1873]

Body: thick
Head: semi-broad
Colour:

    Body – pale to medium brown, creamish-yellow to dark
        chocolate with ragged-edged blotches and spots

    Head – creamish to dark brown with a dark streak from the
        side of the head through the eye

    Belly – cream to white

    Eyes – a dark streak through the eye

Length: up to 1.5 metres; average 0.75 metres
Non-venomous: not dangerous
Habitat: coastal forests to dry woodlands
Young: egg laying

Description:

The Spotted Python is a nocturnal snake found in trees, shrubs or on the ground. It feeds on small mammals, birds and reptiles and can often be found around sheds, gardens and in house roofs. Often mistaken for a Children's Python, it is one of Australia's smallest pythons.

Stimson's Python

Antaresia stimsoni

Also known as **Large-blotched Python**
Family: *Boidae*
Genus: *Antaresia*
[Smith, 1985]

Body: thick
Head: semi-broad
Colour:

    Body – light to dark brown, orange to a reddish colour with irregular, smooth or jagged-edged blotches, or a series of bars on the back and sides which can give a banded effect

    Head – same as body but with smaller blotches

    Belly – white to creamish yellow

    Eyes – orange or brown streak through the eye

Length: up to 1.2 metres; average 0.75 metres
Non-venomous: not dangerous
Habitat: arid environments
Young: egg laying

Description:
A nocturnal snake, the Stimson's Python feeds on small mammals, birds, frogs and lizards, seeking shelter during the day in crevices and cracks to avoid the intense heat. Often mistaken for a Children's Python, but it tends to have a larger snout.

Amethystine Python

Morelia amethistina

Also known as **Scrub Python**
Family: *Boidae*
Genus: *Morelia*
[Schneider, 1801]

Body: long and slender
Head: long and elongated
Colour:
  Body – olive-yellow to olive-green with an iridescent look in the sunlight
  Head – uniform with brown or black spots or streaks
  Belly – cream or yellow
  Eyes – a dark streak through each eye
Length: up to 9 metres; average 5.5 metres
Non-venomous: not dangerous
Habitat: from rainforest to scrubland
Young: egg laying

Description:
Australia's largest snake, the Amethystine Python feeds on fruit bats, possums and birds, and has been known to eat small kangaroos. It first bites its prey, then coils itself around the prey and squeezes before swallowing it whole and headfirst. In the cooler months it lives in open areas basking in the sun, moving to shady forest areas in the warmer months. Mostly a ground dweller, it has also been spotted in trees, and can occasionally be encountered in backyards, sheds and roofs.

Diamond Python

Morelia spilota spilota

Family: *Boidae*
Genus: *Morelia*
[Lacepede, 1804]

Body: heavy
Head: broad
Colour:
    Body – glossy olive-black with cream or yellow spots forming a
           variegated pattern
    Head – lips cream, barred with black
    Belly – cream or yellow
Length: up to 5 metres; average 2 metres
Non-venomous: not dangerous
Habitat: can live in various conditions, from rainforest to desert
Young: egg laying

Description:

In many areas, the Diamond Python lives in the burrows of other animals.
It preys on small mammals, frogs and lizards, sheltering by day in logs,
rock crevices and occasionally in sheds and attics. It is able to kill and eat
anything up to the size of brush-tailed possums and full-grown chickens.
It devours prey headfirst. Pythons stay with their eggs until birth, warming
them by a type of shivering.

Carpet Python

Morelia spilota

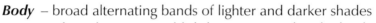

Family: *Boidae*
Genus: *Morelia*
[Lacepede, 1804]

Body: heavy
Head: broad
Colour:
  Body – broad alternating bands of lighter and darker shades
       of tan, brown or reddish-brown (coastal and inland pythons
       can differ in colour variations
  Head – same as body
  Belly – white or cream
Length: up to 5.5 metres; average 2 metres
Non-venomous: not dangerous
Habitat: common in heavily timbered country
Young: egg laying

Description:
Nocturnal, a Carpet Python shelters by day within hollow logs and rock crevices. Also occasionally seen basking in trees, it may hiss if threatened. It feeds on small mammals, frogs and lizards and has been known to enter buildings in search of prey. The scientific name represents its variety of colours. Old skin is shed regularly in one unbroken and transparent stocking.

33

Keelback Snake

Tropidonophis mairii

Also known as **Freshwater Snake**
Family: *Colubridae*
Genus: *Tropidonophis*
[Gray, 1841]

Body: slim to medium
Head: narrow
Colour:
>   *Body* – olive, brown, reddish, grey, mustard yellow –
>   lighter-coloured specimens often have dark spots
>   *Head* – slightly different colour than body
>   *Belly* – cream, olive or salmon

Length: up to 0.8 metres; average 0.5 metres
Non-venomous: not dangerous
Habitat: close to streams, swamps and lagoons
Young: egg laying

Description:
The Keelback Snake is Australia's only non-venomous aquatic snake. It can remain submerged for quite a while. Each scale has a ridge, giving it a rough texture to grip slippery surfaces. It can at times be confused with the venomous Rough-scaled Snake. It usually hunts at night, feeding on frogs and fish. During the day, it shelters under fallen timber, leaf litter or in empty burrows. If threatened, it will raise its head and forebody, then flatten its neck and lunge at the attacker. It may also release an unpleasant odour from its anal gland and discard its tail in order to flee. It has been known to feed on cane toads.

Brown Tree Snake

Boiga irregularis

Family: *Colubridae*
Genus: *Boiga*
[Merrem, 1802]

Body: slim, whip like
Head: broad
Colour:
   Body – tan to reddish-brown with darker cross-bands
   Head – same as body
   Belly – cream to salmon
   Eyes – very large with vertical elliptical pupils
Length: up to 2.4 metres; average 1.2 metres
Venomous: not dangerous
Habitat: humid coastal
Young: egg laying

Description:
Very aggressive when aroused, the Brown Tree Snake throws the front of its body into an S-shaped loop from which it strikes accurately and savagely. This tree-dweller preys on small mammals, birds, eggs and lizards. It is a notorious bird thief and is known to invade domestic birdcages. During World War II it was introduced into Guam, where it is now a major pest problem. It is credited with the extinction of some of Guam's native bird species.

Green Tree Snake

Dendrelaphis punctulata

Also known as **Common Tree Snake**
Family: *Colubridae*
Genus: *Dendrelaphis*
[Gray, 1827]

Body: slim
Head: narrow
Colour:
> *Body* – green, olive, brown, black, sometimes blue
> *Head* – usually darker than body
> *Belly* – white to yellow, green or bluish

Length: up to 1.5 metres; average 1.2 metres
Non-venomous: not dangerous
Habitat: well-timbered areas
Young: egg laying

Description:
Although not dangerous, care should be taken not to confuse this snake with the deadly Eastern Brown. Very agile, it is the most abundant and widely spread of all the tree snakes, and shelters in rock crevices and hollow branches. It spends most of the day in trees and shrubs. It sometimes enters homes in search of prey. It will eat frogs alive and headfirst. When aroused, it flattens its head and forebody to appear larger. When handled, this snake can produce an unpleasant odour.

Death Adders

Common (Southern)

Family: *Elapidae*
Genus: *Acanthophis*
[Daudin, 1803]

Body: fat body tapers to a thin curved spine at the end of the tail
Head: wide flat head tapering to a blunt snout
Colour:

Body – colours vary from light brown to reddish and sometimes black, sometimes banded – tail tip usually white or cream – scales are usually slightly keeled

Head – same as body

Belly – creamish grey with pink or brown blotches

Eyes – small, brown and inconspicuous with a vertical pupil

Length: up to 1.1 metres; average 65 centimetres
Venomous: antivenom Death Adder; dangerous
Habitat: warm dry climate
Young: live bearing

Desert

... cont'd

37

Description:

Also found in New Guinea, the Death Adder is secretive and well camouflaged. It does not frighten easily, and instead of slipping away as a human approaches, it lies motionless and camouflaged. This makes it easy to tread on, which is how most people get bitten. It is unlikely to strike unless touched, but has a very fast strike and tends to hang on. Its fangs are quite long, 6 to 8 millimetres, and it is more mobile than most other venomous snakes. Before antivenom, fifty per cent of bites were fatal. This snake is mostly active at night. It uses its tail like a worm to lure its prey. It spends most of its time half-buried, waiting to ambush prey.

The Northern Death Adder and the Desert Death Adder are both smaller in size than the Common Death Adder. The Desert Death Adder also has a blackish tail tip and the lighter crossbands may have their hind edges marked by black-tipped scales.

Common (Southern)
Acanthophis antarcticus

Desert
Acanthophis pyrrhus

Northern
Acanthophis praelongus

Northern

Copperheads

Lowland Copperhead – *Austrelaps superbus*
Pygmy Copperhead – *Austrelaps labialis*
Highland Copperhead – *Austrelaps ramsayi*
Also known as **Proper Copperheads,**
Diamond or **Superb Snake**
Family: *Elapidae*
Genus: *Austrelaps*
[Gunther, 1858]

Body: heavy
Head: narrow light scales above the mouth often give a striped appearance
Colour:
>   ***Body*** – grey, brassy, copper, russet, brown or black – cream yellow or red along sides
>   ***Head*** – same as body
>   ***Belly*** – yellowish, cream or grey

Length: up to 1.8 metres; average 1.3 metres
Venomous: antivenom Tiger Snake; dangerous
Habitat: cool to cold climates, swampy areas
Young: live bearing

Description:
The Copperhead enjoys cold climates and is the last to begin hibernation and the first one to finish. It is the only venomous snake to be found above the snow line. Not easily aroused, it is generally slow to strike; bites are rare and inaccurate as it often misses. It hunts by day, except in hot weather, and preys on small mammals, lizards and frogs. It frequently eats other snakes, including its own young.

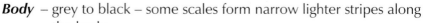

White-crowned Snake

Cacophis harriettae

Family: *Elapidae*
Genus: *Cacophis*
[Krefft, 1869]

Body: slim
Head: narrow
Colour:
> *Body* – grey to black – some scales form narrow lighter stripes along the body
> *Head* – white, cream or yellowish stripe forming a crown
> Belly – dark grey

Length: up to 0.5 metres; average 0.25 metres
Venomous: not dangerous
Habitat: moist forested areas
Young: egg laying

Description:
When threatened, the head of the White-crowned Snake is raised and it mock-strikes – this is essentially a bluff, as it rarely actually strikes. It hunts by night, feeding mainly on lizards. It hides during the day under leaf litter and fallen timber. Often found in suburban gardens, it is seen in the suburbs of Brisbane where it likes to hide in compost heaps and garden beds. Sometimes mistaken for the baby Eastern Brown Snake, it is a capable climber and is the most encountered of the crowned snakes.

Dwarf—crowned Snake

Cacophis krefftii

Also known as: **Krefft's Dwarf Snake**
Family: *Elapidae*
Genus: *Cacophis*
[Gunther, 1863]

Body: slender
Head: narrow
Colour:
    Body – brownish-black to greyish-black
    Head – black with stripe of usually yellow or cream forming a crown
    Belly – white or cream with dark edges
Length: up to 0.5 metres; average 0.2 metres
Venomous: not dangerous
Habitat: forested areas
Young: egg laying

Description:
When threatened, the Dwarf-crowned Snake raises its head and mock-strikes, flicking its tongue, trying to be as threatening as possible. It hunts at night and its prey mainly consists of lizards. It is often found in suburban gardens. Resting by day under rocks, logs and leaf litter, it is the smallest of all the crowned snakes and is a capable tree climber.

Golden-crowned Snake

Cacophis squamulosus

Family: *Elapidae*
Genus: *Cacophis*
[Dumeril, Bibron and
Dumeril, 1854]

Body: slim
Head: narrow
Colour:
>   *Body* – glossy dark brown to grey
>   *Head* – light fawn, yellowish or brown stripe forming a crown
>   *Belly* – bright pink to red with black patches – black stripe under tail
>   *Eyes* – fairly small with vertically elliptic pupil

Length: up to 0.75 metres; average 0.45 metres
Venomous: not dangerous
Habitat: moist forested areas
Young: egg laying

Description:
Not dangerous, but when threatened, the Golden-crowned Snake raises its head and mock-strikes, flicking its tongue to appear as threatening as possible. It will bite if provoked. It hunts by night and its prey mainly consists of lizards. It rests during the day under fallen logs, stones and leaf litter. Often found in suburban gardens, it is a capable tree climber.

Eastern Small-eyed Snake

Cryptophis nigrescens

Also known as **Small-eyed Snake**
Family: *Elapidae*
Genus: *Cryptophis*
[Worrell, 1961]

Body: slim
Head: narrow
Colour:
  Body – glossy black or dark grey, sometimes with bluish tint
  Head – darker than body
  Belly – cream to pink-reddish
Length: up to 0.5 metres; average 0.3 metres
Venomous: dangerous
Habitat: found in many habitats from coastal to forest
Young: live bearing

Description:
Very private, this snake is active during the night. If disturbed, it will thrash about wildly and deliver a bite if provoked. It mainly feeds on lizards and other snakes. Found during the day under stones, logs, crevices and even in the backyard compost heap or bin, it is known to be responsible for at least one human death. It can often be found in grazing land. Combat between the males during the mating season has been observed.

Black Whip Snake

Demansia atra

Family: *Elapidae*
Genus: *Demansia*
[Macleay, 1884]

Body: slender
Head: narrow
Colour:
    Body – olive brown to reddish brown and black
    Head – same as body
    Belly – creamy yellow to greenish grey. Underside of tail reddish
Length: up to 1.5 metres; average 1 metre
Venomous: not dangerous
Habitat: dry sandy country
Young: egg laying

Description:
Only large specimens of this nervous snake are considered dangerous to humans. It feeds mainly on smaller vertebrates and especially lizards. It is very quick and can chase at very high speeds. It shelters under leaf litter, logs and stones while inactive. Males have been observed in combat during the mating season.

Yellow—faced Whip Snake

Demansia psammophis

Family: *Elapidae*
Genus: *Demansia*
[Schlegel, 1837]

Body: slender
Head: narrow
Colour:
  Body – variable in colour from grey to green to brown
  Head – a narrow dark bar around the eyes and to the nostril
  Belly – grey-green to yellow
Length: up to 1.2 metres; average 0.8 metres
Venomous: not dangerous
Habitat: wide range: from rainforest to arid desert
Young: egg laying

Description:

Only the larger specimens of the Yellow-faced Whip Snake are considered dangerous to humans. Very quick, its prey consists of lizards and small vertebrates. Its resting places are usually under rocks, leaf litter or logs. It is sometimes confused with the Eastern Brown Snake. It has good eyesight and is capable of chasing and killing lizards while on the run. It relies on its speed to escape when cornered. A large number will gather in the same area during the mating season.

De Vis Banded Snake

Denisonia devisi

Family: *Elapidae*
Genus: *Denisonia*
[Waite and Longman, 1920]

Body: short, squat with spinous tail tip
(similar to Death Adder)
Head: wide
Colour:
   Body – light brown with dark brown bands which are about twice
       as wide as the lighter bands – the darker scales often have
       lighter brown centres
   Head – dark brown with lighter brown spots, lips barred
   Belly – cream or white
Length: up to 0.5 metres; average 0.35 metres
Venomous: potentially dangerous
Habitat: usually thick vegetation
Young: live bearing

Description:
This snake hunts by night and its prey consists of lizards and frogs. It will
depress its body and hold itself in stiff curves and thrash about if threatened. During the day it will shelter under rocks and leaf litter. It is known
as an ambush hunter and may lie in wait for hours to capture its prey.

White-lipped Snake

Drysdalia coronoide

Family: *Elapidae*
Genus: *Drysdalia*
[Gunther, 1858]

Body: medium
Head: medium
Colour:

  Body – colours vary in shades of grey, brown or reddish – juveniles are black, often peppered by pink

  Head – a black streak runs around the head through the eye with narrow white streak along the upper lip

  Belly – cream, pink or yellow

Length: up to 0.5 metres, average 0.35 metres
Venomous: not dangerous
Habitat: mountainous forests and water-soaked areas
Young: live bearing

Description:
Active during both day and night, but mostly nocturnal, this snake hunts primarily for small skinks. It will bite if handled. Commonly found hidden under stones or logs, it is very common in the Dandenong Ranges of Victoria. It is also the smallest snake found in Tasmania. It is shy and will usually hide at the approach of humans.

Red-naped Snake

Furina diadema

Family: *Elapidae*
Genus: *Furina*
[Schlegel, 1837]

Body: slender
Head: narrow
Colour:

> ***Body*** – reddish-brown, each scale has a black outline
>
> ***Head*** – head and neck shiny black with a red or orange oval or diamond shape across the back of the head, and is within the black
>
> ***Belly*** – white or cream

Length: up to 0.5 metres, average 0.3 metres
Venomous: not dangerous
Habitat: found in all types of areas
Young: egg laying

Description:

Venomous but harmless to humans, the Red-naped Snake will raise the forepart of its body high and rigid and strike out with its mouth closed. A secretive snake, it hunts by night feeding on small lizards and skinks. Often found near termites, it hides during the day under rocks, leaf litter, logs and crevices.

Pale-headed Snake

Hoplocephalus bitorquatus

Family: *Elapidae*
Genus: *Hoplocephalus*
[Jan, 1859]

Body: stocky
Head: wide
Colour:
    Body – uniformly light grey or brown
    Head – dark with cream or white spots
    Belly – creamy grey, sometimes darker spots towards rear
    Eyes – elliptical pupils
Length: up to 1 metre; average 0.5 metres
Venomous: antivenom Tiger Snake; potentially dangerous
Habitat: from rain or wet forests to drier eucalypt forests
Young: live bearing

Description:

The Pale-headed Snake is a habitual tree climber and may be found in branches basking in the sun. It is active mostly at night and its prey consists of small mammals, birds, frogs and lizards. It will shelter in hollow branches and under loose bark. Described as a nervous snake it will strike quickly if threatened without warning. Its bite is painful but not regarded as lethal. It is endangered in some parts of Australia.

Sydney Broad-headed Snake

Hoplocephalus bungaroides

Also known as **Yellow Spotted Snake**
Family: *Elapidae*
Genus: *Hoplocephalus*
[Schlegel, 1837]

Body: narrow
Head: much wider than the neck
Colour:
>   *Body* – mainly black with narrow irregular yellow bands
>   *Head* – face yellow
>   *Belly* – grey to silver, sometimes with yellow blotches

Length: up to 1.5 metres; average 0.75 metres
Venomous: antivenom Tiger Snake; potentially dangerous
Habitat: dry sandstone country within 250 kilometres of Sydney
Young: live bearing

Description:
The Sydney Broad-headed Snake is usually found among rocks. Bad tempered and quick to attack, it strikes repeatedly and high. The potency of its venom has been likened to that of the Copperhead. Hunting mostly by night, it feeds on small mammals, frogs and lizards. It is often found in the Hawkesbury area. It is Australia's only endangered snake. A breeding program began at the Melbourne Zoo to increase its chances of survival, and in March 2000 nine young were born.

Stephen's Banded Snake

Hoplocephalus stephensii

Family: *Elapidae*
Genus: *Hoplocephalus*
[Krefft, 1869]

Body: stocky
Head: broad and flat
Colour:
> *Body* – light grey to black or dark brown with yellowish or black cross-bands
> *Head* – black with brown crown or cream patch on sides of the neck – lips barred with black and cream
> *Belly* – creamish-yellow with black blotches towards the tail

Length: up to 1 metre; average 0.60 metres
Venomous: antivenom Tiger Snake; dangerous
Habitat: well-forested areas with high rainfall
Young: live bearing

Description:
Bad-tempered if disturbed and quick to attack – the Stephen's Banded Snake's body arches in a tight S-shape and it strikes high, repeatedly and accurately. It preys on lizards, small birds, mice and frogs and is most active at night. It rests in trees, shelters in hollows or under loose bark.

Black Tiger Snake

Notechis ater

Family: *Elapidae*
Genus: *Notechis*
[Krefft, 1866]

Subspecies: Krefft's Tiger Snake, King Island Snake, Peninsula Tiger Snake, Kangaroo Island and Islets Tiger Snake, Western Tiger Snake, Chappell Island Tiger Snake

Body: heavy build
Head: broad head
Colour:
   Body – black or dark brown, faint cream or yellow bands on some western snakes
   Head – same as body
   Belly – grey; sometimes cream, yellow or blue
Length: up to 2.4 metres; average 1.8 metres, Kreffts less than 1 metre, others 1.5 metres
Venomous: antivenom Tiger Snake; very dangerous
Habitat: woodland; has adapted to semi-desert
Young: live bearing

Description:
The main population of this snake is to be found in Tasmania. Both of the Bass Strait species prey on migratory mutton-birds – they raid nesting burrows and eat the chicks. The rest of the year they turn cannibalistic. The Chappell Island Black Tiger Snake is the largest. It is quite placid and will often move just a short distance away when disturbed.

Eastern Tiger Snake

Notechis scutatus

Also known as: **Mainland Tiger Snake**, **Common Tiger Snake**
Family: *Elapidae*
Genus: *Notechis*
[Peters, 1861]

Body: heavy wide build
Head: broad head with a shield-like plate between eyes
Colour:
   Body – background of grey, olive, green or brown sometimes reddish or nearly black, with usually 40 to 50 crossbands of yellow or cream
   Head – same as body
   Belly – cream, yellow, olive or grey
Length: up to 1.8 metres; average 1.2 metres
Venomous: antivenom Tiger Snake, dangerous
Habitat: rainforests, river valleys and floodplains; they favour swampy ground
Young: Live bearing

Description:
The Eastern Tiger Snake is usually only aggressive when aroused – it flattens its head like a Cobra but will hiss before attacking. It will strike flat and low and, if able to get a grip, will pump as much venom as it can in a chewing motion. It is mainly active by day but will hunt at night in hot weather. It is a prolific breeder and, because it lives in densely populated areas, it is the species most likely to be trodden on. It does not flee as soon as it hears humans coming, but will usually allow people to get within a metre or so.

Taipan

Oxyuranus scutellatus

Family: *Elapidae*
Genus: *Oxyuranus*
[Peters, 1867]

Body: long, slim
Head: narrow, coffin shaped
Colour:
  Body – fawn to russet to almost black
  Head – snout or whole head cream
  Belly – cream to yellow, reddish marks towards the throat
  Eyes – orange
Length: up to 3.3 metres; average 2.5 metres
Venomous: antivenom Taipan; dangerous
Habitat: well-grassed tropical woodland to tropical wet
Young: egg laying

Description:

The Taipan is the longest of all Australian venomous snakes and has the largest fangs, which can grow to more than 12 millimetres. Although the Taipan's venom is not the most potent, the amount delivered and the depth it reaches make it dangerous. It is shy and will quickly retreat from humans, but if cornered, it is easy to anger and will attack ferociously.

Fierce Snake

Oxyuranus microlepidotus

Also known as **Small-scaled Snake**,
Western Taipan, Inland Taipan
Family: *Elapidae*
Genus: *Oxyuranus*
[McCoy, 1879]

Body: slim
Head: narrow
Colour:
> **Body** – black brown with dark edged scales giving a speckled
> look – sometimes faintly banded towards tail
> **Head** – with scattered darker flecks
> **Belly** – cream or yellow with darker edges
> **Eyes** – round and contained within a yellow iris

Length: up to 2.5 metres; average 1.7 metres
Venomous: antivenom Taipan; dangerous
Habitat: dry arid areas
Young: egg laying

Description:
There is enough venom in the average milking of this snake to kill 100,000
mice. The venom is fifty times more toxic than the Cobra's. It has very
large fangs and the most potent venom of any land snake. Not easily
aroused, it has retreated from the spread of agriculture and is rarely seen.
It feeds on rats and often occupies its victims' burrows. It is sometimes
seen in saltbush vegetation.

Mulga Snake

Pseudechis australis

Also known as **King Brown Snake**
Family: *Elapidae*
Genus: *Pseudechis*
[Gray, 1842]

Body: heavy
Head: broad flat
Colour:

> **Body** – most often copper but varies from light brown to russet, dark olive-brown
>
> **Head** – same as body
>
> **Belly** – pinkish or yellowish cream, sometimes with pink or orange blotches
>
> **Eyes** – brown

Length: up to 3 metres; average 1.5 metres
Venomous: antivenom Black Snake; dangerous
Habitat: from tropical forests to the deserts of the interior
Young: egg laying

Description:

Although it is also known as a King Brown Snake, the Mulga Snake is not a member of the brown snake family. It is found in much the same regions as the browns, but its venom is very different. The Mulga Snake is the biggest of Australian venomous snakes and has the largest output of venom, which makes it highly dangerous. In most cases the venom affects the muscles – causing paralysis, but not affecting the nervous system. It shelters under fallen trees or in rabbit or goanna burrows. It is slow moving and unlikely to bite.

Collett's Snake

Pseudechis colletti

Family: *Elapidae*
Genus: *Pseudechis*
[Boulenger, 1902]

Body: heavy
Head: narrow
Colour:
- *Body* – brown or black with irregular bands of cream or pink – sides often predominantly cream or pink
- *Head* – same as body colour
- *Belly* – creamy yellow or orange

Length: up to 2 metres; average 1.25 metres
Venomous: antivenom Tiger Snake; dangerous
Habitat: found in dry non-swampy ground
Young: egg laying

Description:
Seldom seen by humans, the Collett's Snake lives a virtually subterranean existence, although it can be seen during rat plagues. Male combat has been observed in this species with the usual wrestling, and some have been known to bite each other. When threatened, it flattens its head and forebody and will make several mock strikes before biting. There are no records to show that this snake has ever bitten anyone, but the venom is likened to that of the Mulga Snake. It hunts by day and its prey consists of small mammals, frogs and birds. A rare and threatened species.

Blue—bellied Black Snake

Pseudechis guttatus

Also known as **Spotted Black Snake**
Family: *Elapidae*
Genus: *Pseudechis*
[De Vis, 1909]

Body: heavy
Head: narrow, flat
Colour:
- **Body** – usually glossy black, sometimes dark brown with single cream spots on some scales
- **Head** – same or darker than the body
- **Belly** – bluish grey, sometimes with yellow spots

Length: up to 2 metres; average 1.25 metres
Venomous: antivenom Tiger Snake; dangerous
Habitat: rocky hillsides to river plains and coastal
Young: egg laying

Description:

The Blue-bellied Black Snake is shy, avoids contact where possible and seldom bites; displays of aggression, when it raises its head and forebody, flattens its neck and hisses, are usually a bluff. However, it has been known to bite. It is a day-time hunter, except in hot weather. Its diet consists of small mammals, frogs, lizards and sometimes other snakes. It is the most toxic of all the black snakes. Juveniles have pronounced speckles, but these fade with age. It frequently uses deserted burrows.

Red-bellied Black Snake

Pseudechis porphyriacus

Also known as **Common Black Snake**
Family: *Elapidae*
Genus: *Pseudechis*
[Shaw, 1794]

Body: heavy
Head: narrow
Colour:
  Body – shiny blue-black, lower sides bright red to orange or pink
  Head – blue-black, often light brown
  Belly – dull red or pink, northern species much paler to almost
    white, under tail black
Length: up to 2.5 metres; average 1.25 metres
Venomous: antivenom Tiger Snake; dangerous
Habitat: damp coastal forests and inland river margins
Young: live bearing

Description:
The Red-bellied Black Snake is not an aggressive snake, but will bite. It is
a day-time hunter, except in hot weather. It will often take to water and
lie still like a stick, where it will supplement its diet of mice with fish, eels
and crustaceans. It is also a cannibal and has been known to eat snakes
almost as big as itself. Males are often seen in combat during the mating
season. They will coil their bodies together, each trying to raise its head
above the other. Quick to flee if disturbed; if cornered, it will raise its head
and hiss before striking. Due to the number of cane toads, this species has
decreased in the north.

Dugite

Pseudonaja affinis

Also known as **Spotted Brown Snake**
Family: *Elapidae*
Genus: *Pseudonaja*
[Gunther, 1872]

Body: slender
Head: narrow
Colour:
> *Body* – black, olive or dark brown speckled with black
> *Head* – often lighter than the body, with scales on the back forming a V or W
> *Belly* – yellowish cream or olive with grey or pinkish spots

Length: up to 1.8 metres; average 1.5 metres
Venomous: antivenom Brown Snake; dangerous
Habitat: sandy country
Young: egg laying

Description:
A member of the brown snake family, the Dugite is more aggressive and excitable than other brown snakes. It feeds on mice, hunts during the day and is often found in sheds. It is responsible for the greatest number of snakebites in Western Australia. It has also been known to enter homes through drainage systems. Males bite more frequently than the females. Juveniles are always born with part of their head black.

Speckled Brown Snake

Pseudonaja guttata

Also known as **Spotted Brown Snake**
Family: *Elapidae*
Genus: *Pseudonaja*
[Parker, 1926]

Body: slender
Head: small flattened
Colour:
  Body – creamy brown to salmon flecked by many dark-edged
      scales, sometimes with dark cross-bands
  Head – same as body
  Belly – creamy yellow blotched with orange
Length: up to 1.4 metres; average 1.25 metres
Venomous: antivenom Brown Snake; dangerous
Habitat: anything from dry to wet
Young: egg laying

Description:

A common snake, the Speckled Brown Snake has adapted to a wide variety of climates from drought to flood. When the soil is dry it shelters in
deep cracks in the earth. It preys during the day and feeds on lizards, frogs
and small mammals. Most of their natural habitat is disappearing due to
land clearance for cattle farming.

Ringed Brown Snake

Pseudonaja modesta

Family: *Elapidae*
Genus: *Pseudonaja*
[Gunther, 1872]

Body: slim
Head: narrow
Colour:
   Body – reddish-brown, olive-brown, grey-brown with evenly
      spaced narrow black bands across body and tail – these
      stripes disappear with age
   Head – black with lighter colouring on snout
   Belly – cream with orange blotches
Length: up to 0.7 metres; average 0.45 metres
Venomous: not dangerous
Habitat: arid sandy conditions
Young: egg laying

Description:
The Ringed Brown Snake is the smallest of the brown snakes. There are
usually about five bands on this snake but it may have up to 12. It is active
during both day and night. It shelters in lizard burrows and preys mainly
upon skinks. Although not easily aroused or prone to bite, it should be
treated with respect. It is most commonly found on rocky outcrops and
in dry watercourses.

Gwardar

Pseudonaja nuchalis

Also known as **Western Brown**, **Collared Brown**
Family: *Elapidae*
Genus: *Pseudonaja*
[Gunther, 1858]

Body: slender
Head: narrow
Colour:
    Body – variable from olive-grey to shades of brown or nearly black, may also have dark cross-bands irregular in shape
    Head – often black scales forming a V or W pattern
    Belly – yellowish cream with orange or grey darker blotches
Length: up to 1.8 metres; average 1.4 metres
Venomous: antivenom Brown Snake; dangerous
Habitat: deserts, tropical woodlands
Young: egg laying

Description:
The Gwardar is one of Australia's deadliest, most abundant and widely found snakes; however, it has little contact with humans. If threatened, it is quick to bite. Its venom is less toxic than that of the Eastern Brown. It hunts by night in the north and by day in the south. It is very quick. Combat between males has been observed during mating season. It feeds on small rodents and lizards.

Eastern Brown Snake

Pseudonaja textilis

Also known as **Common Brown Snake**
Family: *Elapidae*
Genus: *Pseudonaja*
[Dumeril, Bibron and Dumeril, 1854]

Body: slender
Head: narrow
Colour:
> *Body* – uniform in shades of grey, brown, orange russet or nearly black, sometimes with very faint narrow cross-bands
> *Head* – same as body, occasionally darker, juveniles have a distinct black area
> *Belly* – cream, yellow or light brown with dark blotches

Length: up to 2.4 metres; average 1.8 metres
Venomous: antivenom Brown Snake; dangerous
Habitat: varies from dry rocky, coastal wet, to inland grasslands
Young: egg laying

Description:
When provoked, an Eastern Brown Snake can thrust a third of its body like a spring. The output of venom is low but it is high in toxicity (second only to the Fierce Snake). Sheltering in burrows of other animals, logs or rocks, it hunts mice, rats and lizards during the day, even in hot weather. It is very fast and very accurate. Juveniles have different colourings, but all have a blackish head and banding on the nape. By the age of three the bands disappear.

Coral Snake

Simoselaps australis

Family: *Elapidae*
Genus: *Simoselaps*
[Kreft, 1864]

Body: slim
Head: narrow
Colour:
> *Body* – pink to red with irregular cross-bands made up of scales
> with cream or yellow centres and dark brown edges
>
> *Head* – a black bar across the head enclosing the eyes and another
> black band at the nape of the neck
>
> *Belly* – cream to yellowish

Length: up to 0.5 metres; average 0.3 metres
Venomous: not dangerous
Habitat: wide range from coastal forest to grassland
Young: egg laying

Description:
The Coral Snake is small and venomous, but harmless. Females are larger than the males and they both have an upturned nose. Not often encountered; it is nocturnal. It shelters during the day under leaf litter, logs and stones and it can be found on the surface on warm nights. It feeds on lizards.

Half-girdled Snake

Simoselaps semifasciatus

Also known as: **Shovel-nosed Snake**
Family: *Elapidae*
Genus: *Simoselaps*
[Gunther, 1863]

Body: slim
Head: small and narrow
Colour:
  Body – pale fawn to olive brown to reddish brown, with many
        darker cross-bands – the paler scales are often dark edged
  Head – blackish bar across the top of the head, enclosing the eyes
  Belly – light cream to grey
Length: up to 0.4 metres; average 0.3 metres
Venomous: not dangerous
Habitat: wide variety from arid to coastal
Young: egg laying

Description:
A small venomous snake with a shovel-shaped snout, the Half-girdled
Snake has a small head and is not much of a threat. It feeds at night on
reptiles' eggs. It is often found foraging on the surface on warm nights. This
burrowing snake shelters during the day under logs, stones and rubbish.

Myall Snake

Suta suta

Also known as: **Curl Snake**
Family: *Elapidae*
Genus: *Suta*
[Peters, 1863]

Body: slim
Head: narrow
Colour:
> *Body* – pale fawn to reddish-brown, edge of scale darker, forming a reticulated pattern
> *Head* – with darker hood
> *Belly* – creamy-white

Length: up to 0.6 metres; average 0.4 metres
Venomous: potentially dangerous
Habitat: from grasslands to woodland
Young: live bearing

Description:
Widely distributed throughout two-thirds of the country, the Myall Snake is nocturnal, feeding on lizards and small mammals. It can be found during the day under logs, stones and leaf litter. Its offensive posture is a spring-like curving of the body. Its bite is not normally regarded as dangerous, but can be painful.

Rough-scaled Snake

Tropidechis carinatus

Also known as **Clarence River Snake**
Family: *Elapidae*
Genus: *Tropidechis*
[Krefft, 1863]

Body: heavy
Head: large
Colour:
> *Body* – greenish brown with dark, narrow irregular cross-bands which do not extend past the belly
> *Head* – same as body
> *Belly* – creamy yellow or olive with blotches of dark green

Length: up to 1 metre; average 0.75 metres
Venomous: antivenom Tiger Snake; dangerous
Habitat: found in moist water areas and forested country
Young: live bearing

Description:
This shy snake is very aggressive when aroused, hissing loudly and lunging to attack when approached. Predominantly a ground dweller, it will climb up trees and over rocks to forage. It is active more often in the evening, especially in warm weather, and will hunt small frogs, mammals and lizards. It is similar in appearance to the Keelback Snake.

Little Whip Snake

Unechis flagellum

Family: *Elapidae*
Genus: *Unechis*
[McCoy, 1878]

Body: slim
Head: narrow
Colour:
   Body – browns to greys to reddish browns – each scale usually
      has a darker edge
   Head – head and nape glossy black, with a bar that extends across
      the snout between the eye and the nostril
   Belly – cream, white to brown
Length: up to 0.6 metres; average 0.3 metres
Venomous: not dangerous
Habitat: cooler climates
Young: live bearing

Description:
Little is known of this species. It feeds on lizards and insects and is a
nocturnal hunter; it is often mistaken for a juvenile Brown Snake. Not
very fast moving, it will adopt a defensive pose if threatened. It raises the
forepart of its body, expands its head and neck, then thrashes its body in a
whip-like fashion. It may emit an unpleasant odour from its anal gland.

Bandy Bandy

Vermicella annulata

Family: *Elapidae*
Genus: *Vermicella*
[Gray, 1842]

Body: slim
Head: narrow
Colour:
> *Body* – broad black and white rings of similar width circling the
>   entire body from nose to tail
> *Head* – same as body
> *Belly* – same as body

Length: up to 1 metre; average 0.4 metres
Venomous: not dangerous
Habitat: from wet rainforests to sandy deserts
Young: egg laying

Description:
A burrowing snake, the Bandy Bandy is infrequently encountered but easily recognised. If threatened, it will flatten itself while arching one or two loops of its body as a show of defence, maintaining this for a while. Not known to bite. Its prey consists of worms. Nocturnal, it hides during the day under stones, rocks or logs, especially after heavy rains.

PART 3

SNAKE TRIVIA

Snake trivia

- There are 140 snake species in Australia.

- Green Tree Snakes come in a variety of colours from black, brown to yellow, and even pale blue.

- The Fierce Snake is the most venomous snake in the world – fortunately it is not aggressive.

- The largest Australian python is the Scrub Python, which grows up to eight metres.

- Live bearing snakes are known as viviparous.

- Egg laying snakes are known as oviparous.

- Some snakes can burrow, all can swim, some climb and some crawl. There is even a group in Asia that can flatten themselves out and glide from tree to tree.

- Snakes from different countries need to be handled differently. Snakes from North America move quickly but strike slowly. Australian snakes move slowly but strike quickly.

- One Anaconda in captivity did not eat for over two years.

- Snakes are not slimy.

- Thirty-four deaths occurred in Australia from snakebites between 1980 and 2000.

- There are over 50 different kinds of Rattlesnake.

- The largest snake in the world is the Anaconda. The largest on scientific record is 12 metres, but there have been sightings of over 20 metres.

The smallest snake in Australia is the Flower Pot Snake at only 12 centimetres.

The heaviest snake in Australia is the King Brown.

The longest Australian snake is the Taipan.

The largest litter ever to be recorded in Australia was that of a Tiger Snake with 109 young.

While looking for a mate, a snake can travel up to half a kilometre a night.

Snakes sometimes change colour with the season.

The fear of snakes is called ophidiophobia.

The forked tongue is a sensory organ used to detect prey.

Snakes do not have ears – they sense vibrations through the ground.

Only about ten per cent of newborn snakes survive.

Eighty per cent of snakebites occur while people are trying to catch or kill the snake.

The Russell's Viper and the Carpet Viper may be responsible for up to 20,000 deaths a year worldwide.

Deadliest snakes

People often wonder what the deadliest snakes are. There are three ways this can be measured:

1. By the greatest number of people killed.

2. By the amount of venom.

3. By the toxicity of the poison.

It is estimated that throughout the world there are at least one million people bitten by snakes every year. Of those, at least 50,000 are fatalities.

The country with the highest rate of snakebite fatalities is Sri Lanka.

In the United States there are approximately 45,000 incidents, but only nine to 15 fatalities each year.

The Asian Cobra and the Russell's Viper probably kill more people than any other snakes, but neither would make it into the top ten most toxic.

The deadliest snake in Australia would be the Eastern Brown Snake, responsible for 22 of the last 37 deaths.

The fifteen worst snakes

This list is a popular version. No two lists anywhere are the same, so a compilation of many has been taken.

1. Fierce Snake   Australia
2. Eastern Brown   Australia
3. Taipan   Australia
4. Eastern Tiger   Australia
5. Black Mamba   Africa
6. Saw Scaled Viper   Middle East, Asia
7. Death Adder   Australia
8. Gwardar   Australia
9. Copperhead   Australia
10. Boomslang   Africa
11. King Cobra   Asia
12. Dugite   Australia
13. Papuan Black   Papua New Gunea
14. Mulga   Australia
15. Stephen's Banded   Australia

Remember this is not an official list so don't place any bets.

Fierce Snake –
Australia

Index

Emergency contacts

Poisons information centres
13 11 26 (Australia-wide)

Commonwealth Serum Laboratories Ltd
(03) 9389 1911 (All-hours number for referral to a CSL consultant on the use of antivenom and the management of envenoming)

The International Venom and Toxin Database
www.kingsnake.com/toxinology

Photo credits

The publisher would like to thank the following people for the use of photographs in this book:

Ray Hoser:
Children's Python, Amethystine Python, Diamond Python, Keelback Snake, Green Tree Snake, Death Adders, Copperhead, White Crowned Snake, Dwarf-crowned Snake, Golden-crowned Snake, Eastern Small-eyed Snake, Black Whip Snake, Yellow-faced Whip Snake, De Vis Banded Snake, White-lipped Snake, Red-naped Snake, Pale-headed Snake, Sydney Broad-headed Snake, Stephen's Banded Snake, Black Tiger Snake, Eastern Tiger Snake, Taipan, Fierce Snake, Collett's Snake, Red-bellied Black Snake, Dugite, Ringed Brown Snake, Gwardar, Eastern Brown Snake, Coral Snake, Half-girdled Snake, Myall Snake, Rough-scaled Snake, Little Whip Snake, Bandy Bandy.

Melbourne Reptile House:
Brown Tree Snake, Carpet Python, Stimson's Python, Spotted Python, Mulga Snake, Collett's Snake, Blue-bellied Black Snake, Speckled Brown Snake.

Visit the Melbourne Reptile House at:
259 Plenty Road, Preston, Vic. 3072
Phone: (03) 9480 2622